Ninja Weapons

Jon M. Fishman

Lerner Publications ◆ Minneapolis

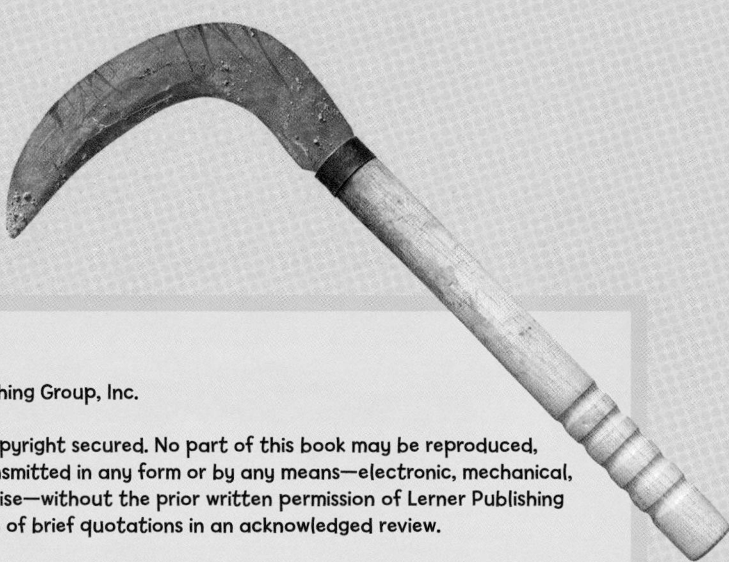

Lerner Publications Company
An imprint of Lerner Publishing Group, Inc.
241 First Avenue North
Minneapolis, MN 55401 USA

For reading levels and more information, look up this title at www.lernerbooks.com.

Library of Congress Cataloging-in-Publication Data

Names: Fishman, Jon M., author.
Title: Ninja weapons / Jon M. Fishman.
Description: Minneapolis : Lerner Publications, [2020] | Series: Lightning bolt books : ninja mania | Includes bibliographical references and index. | Audience: Ages: 6-9 | Audience: Grades: 2-3 | Summary: "Did ninja really use shuriken, or throwing stars? Did female ninja carry fans made of steel? Find out what's myth and what's history as this title explores the tools and weapons of the ninja" —Provided by publisher.
Identifiers: LCCN 2019028050 (print) | LCCN 2019028051 (ebook) | ISBN 9781541577084 (library binding) | ISBN 9781541589179 (paperback) | ISBN 9781541583269 (ebook)
Subjects: LCSH: Ninja—Juvenile literature. | Martial arts weapons—Juvenile literature. | Ninjutsu—Juvenile literature. | Kunoichi—Juvenile literature. | Ninja—Japan—Juvenile literature. | Japan—History, Military—To 1868—Juvenile literature.
Classification: LCC UB271.J3 F57 2020 (print) | LCC UB271.J3 (ebook) | DDC 355.8/241—dc23

LC record available at https://lccn.loc.gov/2019028050
LC ebook record available at https://lccn.loc.gov/2019028051

Manufactured in the United States of America
1-46730-47721-9/4/2019

Table of Contents

Ninja History 4

Tales of Ninja 8

Ninja in Action 12

Ninja Gear 16

Real-Life Ninja 20

Ninja Fun Facts 21

Glossary 22

Further Reading 23

Index 24

Ninja History

A ninja pulls a thin knife from his pocket. He pushes the knife into a lock on a door and twists. The lock breaks and the door swings open. The ninja steps quietly into the castle.

Spies such as ninja have existed for thousands of years. The first ninja appear in Japanese stories more than five hundred years ago.

Unlike the samurai shown here, ninja were so secretive that very little is known about them.

From the mid-fifteenth century to the seventeenth century, powerful Japanese families warred against one another to control the country. Ninja had important roles in these wars.

Ninja spied on enemy troops. They used weapons to destroy enemy supplies. Sometimes, they used weapons to attack enemy soldiers.

Samurai soldiers fought out in the open while ninja worked in secret.

Tales of Ninja

By the seventeenth century, ninja had become less common in Japan. People told stories about them and the weapons they used.

Some stories said that ninja often fought without weapons. They used special kicks and punches to take down enemies. In real life, ninja used many different weapons.

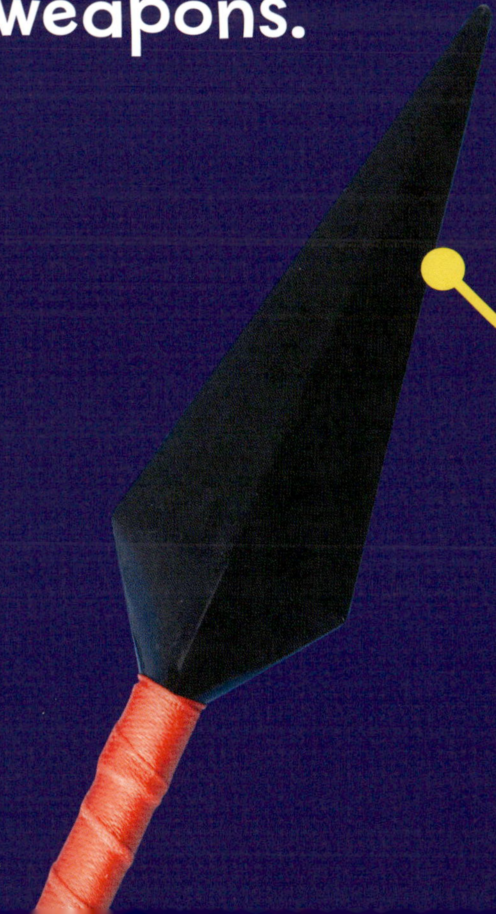

Ninja may have used kunai knives to climb castle walls.

Other myths told of ninja using samurai swords. But only samurai warriors used these weapons. Ninja wanted to stay hidden, and people would notice such a long sword.

Ninja often used smaller weapons than the samurai sword shown here.

The first throwing stars may have been made from sticks or rocks tied together.

Throwing stars are common weapons in ninja myths. But ninja probably didn't throw them at enemies. Instead, they may have thrown them to scare or distract people.

Ninja in Action

A farmer carries a basket to a supply shed. When no one is looking, she uses an explosive to set the building on fire. The farmer is a ninja, and she just destroyed the enemy's food and tools.

To stay hidden from enemies, ninja dressed like people around them. Since many people farmed in the time of the ninja, ninja often dressed as farmers to blend in.

Dressed as farmers, ninja could travel almost anywhere without being noticed.

A sickle is a farm tool used to cut plants. It has a long, curved blade. When ninja dressed as farmers, they often used sickles as weapons.

Ninja used any weapons they needed to complete their missions. They fired guns and even used explosives to blow up enemy buildings and supplies.

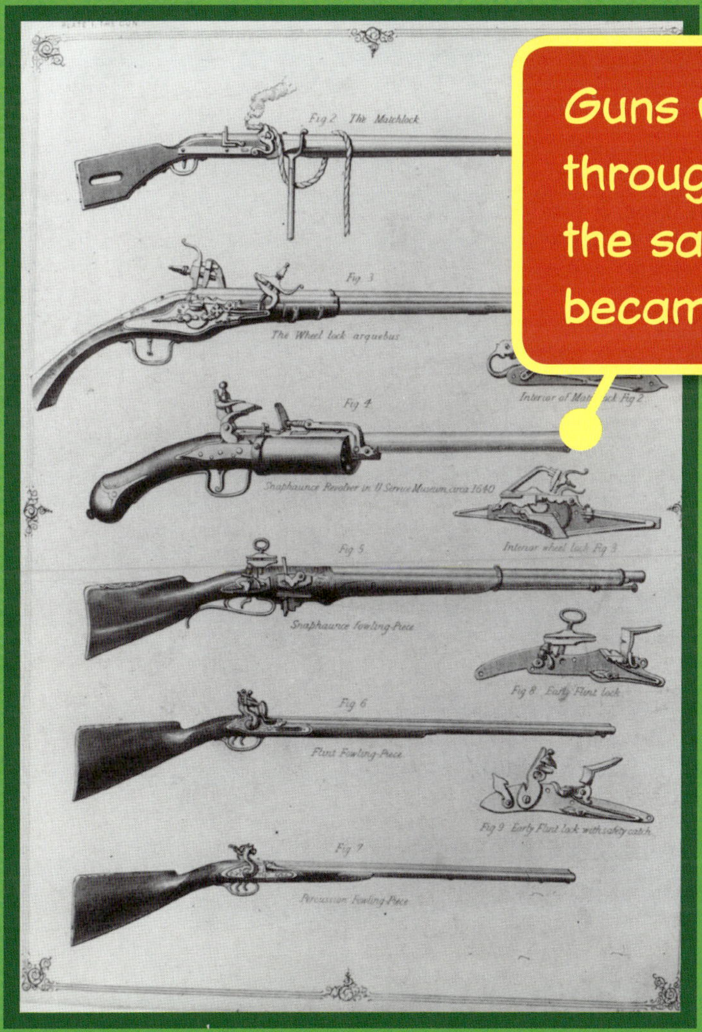

Guns were spreading through Japan around the same time ninja became active.

Ninja Gear

Ninja gear has changed a lot since the seventeenth century. Ninja no longer use farm tools as weapons. High-tech weapons and gear help modern ninja do their jobs.

Instead of dressing like farmers, modern soldiers dress to blend into their surroundings.

Some modern soldiers are like ninja. They serve in armies for the United States and other countries. Special clothing helps them stay hidden.

Soldiers can destroy enemy supplies with high-tech explosives. They carry guns, knives, and other weapons.

Soldiers often carry small knives that they use for many things.

Soldiers can even use some weapons underwater!

Like ninja, soldiers use any weapons they need to do their jobs. High-tech weapons help them win fights and protect their country.

Real-Life Ninja

As with most tales of ninja from Japan's past, many stories about Hattori Hanzo's life are myths. But we know he was the leader of a group of ninja in the sixteenth century. Stories tell of Hanzo and his fellow ninja protecting Tokugawa Ieyasu on a journey as fighting raged around them. Ieyasu later became the leader of Japan.

Hanzo is still famous among ninja fans. Modern ninja movies often include characters based on him. Dozens of video games also feature characters inspired by Hanzo.

Ninja Fun Facts

- Ninja didn't have magical powers. But in myths, they could disappear and attack their enemies with magic. Some stories even said ninja could fly.
- *Shinobi* is another Japanese word for "ninja."
- The skills and methods of ninja are called ninjutsu. Ninjutsu skills include spying, fighting, making medicine, and much more.

Glossary

explosive: a weapon made to explode

high-tech: made with the newest scientific knowledge

modern: from the present time

myth: a story about the past that may not be true

samurai: noble soldiers in Japan who followed strict rules

sickle: a cutting tool with a curved blade and a short handle

spy: to gather information in secret

supply: a tool, food, or other needed material

throwing star: a small, sharp blade shaped like a star

Further Reading

Fishman, Jon M. *Real-Life Ninja.* Minneapolis: Lerner Publications, 2020.

Hansen, Grace. *Japan.* Minneapolis: Abdo Kids, 2019.

Japan
https://kids.nationalgeographic.com/explore/countries/japan/

Ninja Facts for Kids
https://kids.kiddle.co/Ninja

Ninja—Kids Web Japan
https://web-japan.org/kidsweb/explore/history/q4.html

Terp, Gail. *Ninja.* Mankato, MN: Black Rabbit Books, 2020.

Index

explosives, 12, 15, 18

gear, 16

Japan, 5-6, 8

soldiers, 7, 17-19
spy, 5, 7

weapons, 7-11, 14-16, 18-19

Photo Acknowledgments

Image credits: BYUNGSUK KO/Shutterstock.com, p. 2; PamelaJoeMcFarlane/Getty Images, p. 4; BernardAllum/Getty Images, pp. 5, 23; Nattachart Jerdnapapunt/Moment/Getty Image, p. 6; davidf/E+/Getty Images, p. 7; Chasethesonphotography/Moment/Getty Images, p. 8; Nattapol Sritongcom/EyeEm//Getty Images, p. 9; TommasoT/E+/Getty Images, p. 10; Zysko Sergii/Shutterstock.com, p. 11; Susan Dykstra/Design Pics/Getty Images, p. 12; Felice Beato/Alinari/Getty Images, p. 13; Hulton Archive/Getty Images, p. 15; nU.S. Army Photo by Sgt. Alexis K. Washburn, p. 16; U.S. Army Photo by U.S. Army Staff Sgt. Gary A. Witte, 300th Mobile Public Affairs Detachment, p. 17; Becart/Getty Images, p. 18; U.S. Army Photo , p. 19.

Cover: metamorworks/Shutterstock.com.

Main body text set in Billy Infant regular. Typeface provided by SparkType.